disc

WEATHER WATCH

Rain

by Alice K. Flanagan

Drip, drip. Splash! Here comes the rain!

Rain bounces off the ground.

There are many kinds of rainfall. A **sprinkle** is light. A **downpour** is heavy.

Rain comes down hard in a park.

Rain is part of the **water cycle**. How does water become rain? First, the sun heats water in lakes, rivers, and oceans.

The sun heats the water in a lake.

As water heats up, it turns into a **gas**. You cannot see the gas as it rises into the cooler air in the sky. Then the gas cools, too.

Gas rises off the ocean's surface.

The gas turns into tiny drops of water again. The drops form clouds. The drops become too heavy to stay in the air. Then they fall as rain.

Rain clouds gather in the sky.

Rain falls onto the soil. Then it flows into rivers, lakes, and oceans. The water cycle begins again.

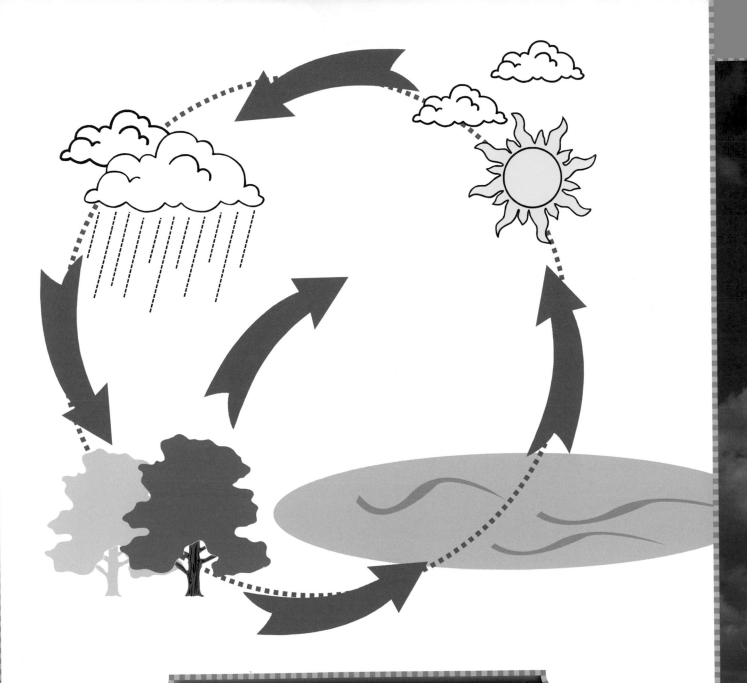

This is a picture of the water cycle.

It takes up to 15 minutes for rain to reach the ground. The time depends on how high the clouds are.

Rain pounds the surface of a lake.

In some places, the rain might not even reach the ground. It dries up before it gets there. This happens when the air near the ground is very warm. The warm air turns the rain back into a gas.

Deserts do not get much rain.

Rain can be good. It helps plants grow. It cleans the air of dust and **pollution**. But too much rain can be bad. It can cause a **flood**. A flood can harm people and animals.

Rain has flooded this road.

The next time it rains, remember that it is all part of the water cycle!

Two girls are caught in the rain.

downpour (DOWN-por): A downpour is a heavy rain. A downpour brings a lot of water.

flood (FLUD): A flood happens when lakes and rivers cannot hold any more water. A flood can harm people's houses.

gas (GASS): A gas is what a liquid turns into when it is heated. The sun turns water into gas.

pollution (puh-LOO-shun): Pollution is material that harms the environment. Rain can help clean pollution out of the air.

sprinkle (SPRING-kul): A sprinkle is a light rain. A sprinkle brings a small amount of water.

water cycle (WAH-tur SYE-kul): The water cycle is the constant movement of Earth's water. Rain is part of the water cycle.

To Find Out More

Books

Bauer, Marion Dane. *Rain*. New York: Simon & Schuster, 2004.

Mara, Wil. *Why Does It Rain?* New York: Benchmark Books, 2009.

Rene, Ellen. *Investigating Why It Rains*. New York: PowerKids Press, 2008.

Web Sites

Visit our Web site for links about rain:
childsworld.com/links

Note to Parents, Teachers, and Librarians: We routinely verify our Web links to make sure they are safe and active sites. So encourage your readers to check them out!

Index

About the Author

Alice K. Flanagan taught elementary school for ten years. She has been writing for more than twenty years. She has written biographies and books about holidays, careers, animals, and weather.

On the cover: Rain falls in a park.

Published by The Child's World®
1980 Lookout Drive • Mankato, MN 56003-1705
800-599-READ • www.childsworld.com

ACKNOWLEDGMENTS
The Child's World®: Mary Berendes, Publishing Director
The Design Lab: Design and production
Red Line Editorial: Editorial direction

PHOTO CREDITS: Sven Klaschik/iStockphoto, cover, 5; iStockphoto, cover, 17, 21; Adam Mandoki/iStockphoto, 3; Slobo Mitic/iStockphoto, 7; Erik Kolstad/iStockphoto, 9; Adrian Assalve/iStockphoto, 11; hkannn/Shutterstock, 13; Henrik Jynnesjö/iStockphoto, 15; Jeremy Wedel/iStockphoto, 19

Printed in the United States of America in Mankato, Minnesota.
November 2009
F11460

LIBRARY OF CONGRESS CATALOGING-IN-PUBLICATION DATA
Flanagan, Alice K.
   Rain / Alice K. Flanagan.
      p. cm. — (Weather watch)
   Includes index.
   ISBN 978-1-60253-361-5 (library bound : alk. paper)
   1. Rain and rainfall—Juvenile literature. I. Title. II. Series.
   QC924.7.F55 2010
   551.57'7—dc22   2009030216